THE BOOK OF
PRAYERS
FOR THE
SEASONS IN LIFE

THE REV. MATTHEW SHANNON, M. DIV.
AUTHOR

The Book of
Prayers
for the
Seasons in Life

The Rev. Matthew Shannon, M. Div.
Author

Ignite Your Core Publishing Company
VIRGINIA BEACH, VA
UNITED STATES

The Book of
Prayers
for the
Seasons in Life

Printed in the United States of America.

Cover photo: Public Domain
The tree experiences four seasons in its life: winter, spring, summer, and
fall. Like the tree, people experience different seasons in life.

ISBN: 978-0615903149

Table of Contents

Table of Contents (Continued)

Acknowledgements

I want to take the time to acknowledge some very special people in my life that have taught me how to pray, encouraged me to pray, and have given me the opportunity to publicly pray. Also, I want to acknowledge a special group of people that prayed for me when I felt like giving up in a tough season in my life.

First, I want to acknowledge my God and my Savior, Jesus Christ who through their Spirit have motivated me to live a life of daily prayer and to share my words and prayers with others.

Second, I want to acknowledge my Mother, Cheryl, my Father, O'Connor, my older brother Tony, and my older sister Tanya who have encouraged me to pray in whatever season I am in...

Third, I want to acknowledge my spiritual mentors, who have taught me valuable lessons on prayer, The Rev. Janice Parker and The Rev. James F. Mason.

Fourth, I want to acknowledge my church families that I have prayed for countless times: St. John African Methodist Episcopal (A.M.E.) Church, St. Louis, MO; St. Peter A.M.E. Church, St. Louis, MO; Bethel A.M.E. Church, Hampton, VA; Flipper Temple A.M.E. Church in Atlanta and St. Mark A.M.E. Church, Virginia Beach, VA.

Last, but not least I want to acknowledge the Anchor Ministry, the young adults of Bethel A.M.E. Church in Hampton, VA. They prayed for me when I was going through a difficult season in my life. Without their support, this book would have been impossible to finish.

Introduction to the
Book of Prayers for the Seasons in Life

"For everything there is a season, and a time for every matter under heaven."
Ecclesiastes 3:1 (NRSV)

On any given day or moment, our lives can change dramatically. We can be depressed in one moment and joyous the next moment. Everything could be going okay in our lives, until a phone call from a family member, or a text message from a friend. When we experience the changes in life or how I would like to call them, the seasons in life, we need to guard ourselves with prayer. Prayer is a conversation between you and God. Prayer is like the engine that starts the car in our relationship with God. When we talk to God, we should expect God to speak back to us. Will God respond to us right after we talk to God? Sometimes God will respond to our plea immediately, but there are seasons when we have to be patient and listen to the sound of God's voice for an answer to our request.

There are different conversations with God that we can have. We can intercede on behalf of others, we can pray for our own struggles, and we can pray a prayer of blessing. In this book, you will find different types of prayers for the seasons that you are going through. In Ecclesiastes, chapter 3, the writer says that there is a season for everything under the sun. In these seasons of life, we need prayer as a driving force in our lives.

When I was 12, I started praying in public. I attended a youth event at church and I was asked to deliver the invocation. I had never prayed before openly, but I just started talking to God like I did in my private times. The Holy Spirit fell on that congregation. Ever since my first public prayer, I've found a passion to pray. When I attended Hampton University, I was honored to serve as the Noonday Prayer Leader for the campus. Every Monday, Wednesday, and Friday, a group of the student body would gather and pray. I discovered that prayer truly works.

One time I went to visit a sick person in the hospital. The person was in ICU (Intensive Care Unit) the doctors had told the person it was only a matter of time before their life was over. I began to pray for them. I asked the person if they wanted to live. They replied, YES! We touched and agreed in the name of Jesus and one week later, the person left the hospital and their body was restored.

Prayer works and it changes things. The Word of God says, the effectual prayers of the righteous person avails much. When you pray to God, God listens and responds to you. It doesn't matter where you are, GOD LISTENS To YOU!

The purpose of this book is to lead you to pray in the various seasons in your life. This book will encourage you to go further in your prayer life and help you to create your own inspiring prayers. I would encourage you to read the prayers out loud, and then read them silently, and then go further within your spirit to pray according to the season you are going through and create your own prayer.

Chapter 1 begins with several famous prayers within the Bible. These would include: The Lord's Prayer, Psalm 23, Nehemiah's Prayer, Hannah's Prayer, and Jesus' Prayers in the Book of John. These prayers teach us how to pray.

Chapter 2 features prayers for special occasions, such as Easter, Christmas, & Valentine's Day.

Chapter 3 includes prayers for the feelings of rejection, guilt, shame, loneliness, depression, grief, and jealousy.

Chapter 4 covers prayers for the human body. This would include seasons of illness and struggles with body image.

Chapter 5 lists prayers for humankind. This includes: African American Men & Women, Children, Singles, and Married Couples.

Chapter 6 features prayers for the seasons in life that come unexpected such as job loss, unplanned pregnancy, crime, and tragedies.

Chapter 7 includes prayers for our leaders in the government, church, community, and schools.

Chapter 8, the final chapter offers prayers to help you as you adjust to a new life. This would include prayers for high school graduates, college graduates, new careers, and prayers of salvation & recommitment.

I hope these prayers will uplift and bless your life and will encourage you to go deeper in your prayer relationship with God.

**Remember this: Much Prayer, Much Power;
Little Prayer, little power; No prayer, no power.**

"But whenever you pray, go into your room and shut the door and pray to your Father who is in secret; and your Father who sees in secret will reward you."
Matthew 6:6 (NRSV)

Chapter One

Biblical Prayers
for the Seasons in Life

The
Lord's Prayer
Matthew 6: 9-13 (KJV)

Our Father, which art in heaven, hallowed be thy name. Thy

kingdom come. Thy will be done, on earth as it is in heaven.

Give us this day our daily bread. And forgive us our trespasses,

as we forgive those who have trespassed against us.

And lead us not into temptation, but deliver us from evil.

For thine is the kingdom, the power, and the glory. AMEN.

King David's
Prayer
Psalm 23 (NKJV)

The Lord is my Shepherd. I shall not want. He makes me lie

down in green pastures; He leads me beside the still waters;

He restores my soul. He leads me in the paths of righteousness

for His name's sake. Yea, though I walk through the valley of the

shadow of death, I will fear no evil; for You are with me; Your

rod and Your staff, they comfort me. You prepare a table before

be in the presence of my enemies; you anoint my head with oil;

my cup overflows. Surely goodness and mercy shall follow me all

the days of my life, and I will dwell in the house of the Lord for-

ever. AMEN.

King David's Prayer of Forgiveness
Psalm 51: 1-13 (NRSV)

Have mercy on me, O God, according to your steadfast love; according to your abundant mercy blot out my transgressions. Wash me thoroughly from my iniquity, and cleanse me from my sin. For I know my transgressions; and my sin is ever before me. Against you, you alone, have I sinned, and done what is evil in your sight, so that you are justified in your sentence and blameless when you pass judgment. Indeed, I was born guilty, a sinner when my mother conceived me. You desire truth in the inward being; therefore teach me wisdom in my secret heart. Purge me with hyssop, and I shall be clean; wash me, and I shall be whiter than snow. Let me hear joy and gladness; let the bones that you have crushed rejoice. Hide your face from my sins, and blot out all my iniquities. Create in me a clean heart, O God, and put a new and right spirit within me. Do not cast me away from your presence, and do not take your holy spirit from me. Restore to me the joy of your salvation, and sustain in me a willing spirit. Then I will teach transgressors your ways, and sinners will return to you. AMEN.

Nehemiah's Prayer

Nehemiah 1:5-11a (NRSV)

O Lord God of heaven, the great and awesome God who keeps covenant and steadfast love with those who love him and keep his commandments; let your ear be attentive and your eyes open to hear the prayer of your servant that I now pray before you day and night for your servants, the people of Israel, confessing the sins of the people of Israel, which we have sinned against you. Both I and my family have sinned. We have offended you deeply, failing to keep the commandments, the statutes, and the ordinances that you commanded your servant Moses. Remember the word that you commanded your servant, Moses, 'If you are unfaithful, I will scatter you among the peoples; but if you return to me and keep my commandments and do them, though your outcasts are under the farthest skies, I will gather them from there and bring them from the place at which I have chosen to establish my name.' They are your servants and your people, whom you redeemed by your great power and your strong hand. O Lord, let your ear be attentive to the prayer of your servant, and to the prayer of your servants who delight in revering your name. Give success to your servant today, and grant him mercy in the sight of this man!" AMEN.

Hannah's Prayer for a Child
1 Samuel 1:11 (NRSV)

O Lord of hosts, if only you will look on the misery of your servant, and remember me, and not forget your servant, but will give to your servant a male child, then I will set him before you as a nazirite until the day of his death. He shall drink neither wine nor intoxicants, and no razor shall touch his head. AMEN.

Hannah's Prayer of Thanksgiving
1 Samuel 2:1-10 (NRSV)

My heart exults in the Lord; my strength is exalted in my God. My mouth derides my enemies, because I rejoice in my victory. There is no Holy One like the Lord, no one besides you; there is no Rock like our God. Talk no more so very proudly, let not arrogance come from your mouth; for the Lord is a God of knowledge, and by him actions are weighed.

The bows of the mighty are broken, but the feeble gird on strength. Those who were full have hired themselves out for bread, but those who were hungry are fat with spoil. The barren has borne seven, but she who has many children is forlorn. The Lord kills and brings to life; he brings down to Sheol and raises up. The Lord makes poor and makes rich; he brings low; he also exalts. He raises up the poor from the dust; he lifts the needy from the ash heap, to make them sit with princes and inherit a seat of honor. For the pillars of the earth are the Lord's, and on them he has set the world. He will guard the foot of his faithful ones, but the wicked shall be cut off in darkness; for not by might does one prevail. The Lord! His adversaries shall be shattered; the Most High will thunder in heaven. The Lord will judge the ends of the earth; he will give strength to his king, and exalt the power of his anointed. AMEN.

Prayer of Jabez
I Chronicles 4:10 (NRSV)

Oh, God of Israel, that you would bless me and enlarge my border, and that your hand might be with me, and that you would keep me from hurt and harm! AMEN.

Deborah's Prayer of Praise
Judges 5:1-5 (NRSV)

"When locks are long in Israel, when the people offer themselves willingly- bless the Lord! Hear, O kings; give ear, O princes; to the Lord I will sing, I will make melody to the Lord, the God of Israel. Lord, when you went out from Seir, when you marched from the region of Edom, the earth trembled, and the heavens poured, the clouds indeed poured water. The mountains quaked before the Lord, the God of Israel." AMEN.

Hezekiah's Prayer to Prolong His Life
Isaiah 38:3 (NRSV)

"Remember me now, O Lord, I implore you, how I have walked before you in faithfulness with a whole heart, and have done what is good in your sight." AMEN.

Stephen's Prayer to Forgive Others
Acts 7:59-60 (NRSV)

"Lord Jesus, receive my spirit.
Lord, do not hold the sin against them." AMEN.

Paul's Prayer
to the Church of Ephesus
Ephesians 1:17-19 (NRSV)

I pray that the God of our Lord Jesus Christ, the Father of glory, may give you a spirit of wisdom and revelation as you come to know him, so that, with the eyes of your heart enlightened, you may know what is the hope to which he has called you, what are the riches of his glorious inheritance among the saints, and what is the immeasurable greatness of his power for us who believe, according to the working of his great power. AMEN.

Paul's Prayer
to the Church of Philippi
Philippians 1:9-11 (NRSV)

And this is my prayer, that your love may overflow more and more with knowledge and full insight to help you to determine what is best, so that in the day of Christ you may be pure and blameless, having produced the harvest of righteousness that comes through Jesus Christ for the glory and praise of God. AMEN.

Paul's Prayer
to the Church of Colossae
Colossians 1:9-14 (NRSV)

I pray that you may be filled with the knowledge of God's will in all spiritual wisdom and understanding, so that you may lead lives worthy of the Lord, fully pleasing to him, as you bear fruit in every good work and as you grow in the knowledge of God. May you be made strong with all the strength that comes from his glorious power, and may you be prepared to endure everything with patience, while joyfully giving thanks to the Father, who has enabled you to share in the inheritance of the saints in the light. He has rescued us from the power of darkness and transferred us into the kingdom of his beloved Son, in whom we have redemption, the forgiveness of sins. AMEN.

Mary, the Mother of Jesus Prayer
Luke 1: 46-55 (NRSV)

My soul magnifies the Lord, and my spirit rejoices in God my Savior, for he has looked with favor on the lowliness of his servant. Surely, from now on all generations will call me blessed; for the Mighty One has done great things for me, and holy is his name. His mercy is for those who fear him from generation to generation. He has shown strength with his arm; he has scattered the proud in the thoughts of their hearts. He has brought down the powerful from their thrones, and lifted up the lowly; he has filled the hungry with good things, and sent the rich away empty. He has helped his servant Israel, in remembrance of his mercy, according to the promise he made to our ancestors, to Abraham and to his descendents forever. AMEN.

Jesus' Prayer for Himself
in Gethsemane
John 17:1-5 (NRSV)

"Father, the hour has come; glorify your Son so that the Son may glorify you, since you have given him authority over all people, to give eternal life to all whom you have given him. And this is eternal life, that they may know you, the only true God, and Jesus Christ whom you have sent. I glorified you on earth by finishing the work that you gave me to do. So, now Father, glorify me in your own presence with the glory that I had in your presence before the world existed."

Jesus' Prayer
for His Disciples
John 17:6-19 (NRSV)

"I have made your name known to those whom you gave me from the world, They were yours, and you gave them to me, and they have kept your word. Now they know that everything you have given me is from you; for the words that you gave to me I have given to them, and they have received them and know in truth that I came from you; and they have believed that you sent me. I am asking on their behalf; I am not asking on behalf of the world, but on behalf of those whom you gave me, because they are yours. All mine are yours, and yours are mine; and I have been glorified in them. And now I am no longer in the world, but they are in the world, and I am coming to you. Holy Father, protect them in your name that you have given me, so that they may be one, as we are one. While I was with them, I protected them in your name that you have given me. I guarded them, and not one of them was lost except the one destined to be lost, so that the scripture might be fulfilled. But now I am coming to you, and I speak these things in the world so that they may have my joy made complete in themselves. I have given them your word, and the world has hated them because they do not belong in the world, just as I do not belong to the world. I am not asking you to take them out of the world, but I ask you to protect them from the evil one. They do not belong to the world, just as I do not belong to the world. Sanctify them in truth; your word is truth. As you have sent me into the world, so I have sent them into the world. And for their sakes I sanctify myself, so that they also may be sanctified in truth."

Jesus' Prayer for the World
John 17:20-26 (NRSV)

"I ask not only on behalf of these, but also on behalf of those who will believe in me through their word, that they may all be one. As you, Father, are in me and I am in you, may they also be in us, so that the world may believe that you have sent me. The glory that you have given me I have given them, so that they may be one, as we are one, I in them and you in me, that they may become completely one, so that the world may know that you have sent me and have loved them even as you have loved me. Father, I desire that those also, whom you have given me because you loved me before the foundation of the world.

Righteous Father, the world does not know you, but I know you; and these know that you have sent me. I made your name known to them, and I will make it known, so that the love with which you have loved me may be in them, and I in them." AMEN.

Chapter Two

Prayers for the Seasons in Life:
Special Occasions

Prayers for the Season of Advent

Dear God, as we anticipate and prepare for the celebration of Jesus coming to the world through the Season of Advent, help us not get into the pains of holiday stress. Rather, let us march forward in our preparation with hope, love, joy, and peace in this Christmas season. Let us focus our hearts and minds on giving hope, love, joy and peace to our neighbors around us—whether in our home, our job, our school, our church, or in our community. Let us be a beacon of light in the midst of darkness, spreading goodwill to those among us. In Your Son's name, we pray. AMEN.

For unto us a son is given...

God, as we wait for the celebration of Christ's Coming to the World, help the young people remember that this is the season of giving. It is the season for Jesus. It is better to give than it is to receive. The coming of Jesus is the Ultimate Gift to humankind. No person can buy any gift greater than the salvation that Jesus provides. So, God, provide our children with gifts, but most importantly, help them to be thankful and give after they have received the gifts during this Christmas Season. As Christians, we can not sit with the gifts that Jesus has given us; we have to use them to God's glory. In Jesus Name, we pray. AMEN.

Prayer for Christmas Day

O what a pretty little baby, in a manger low, wrapped in swaddling clothes didn't come with a fanfare but started in a humble beginning. God, I come to you on this Christmas Day with joy in my heart. God, as I have spent the past four weeks preparing for this day through the season of Advent, help me to truly celebrate this day. Christmas is a time of rejoicing, not a season of depression. If I don't have anybody to share this special day with, help me find a special person to share it with. In Jesus Name, I pray. AMEN.

Prayer for
New Year's Eve

Dear All-Knowing God, you have brought us to the cusp of another year. It is one more year to endure the trials and tribulations of this world. It is one more year to serve and please you. Thank you, God for bringing us this far by faith. Lead us and guide us along the way this next year. We do not know what will happen in this coming year. Forgive us from our sins this past year. Search our heart and mind for things that are not of you. We want to be more like you in this next year. Help us to lead righteous lives in the New Year ahead and bless us with the gift of discernment for any major decisions that we will have to face in this next year. In Jesus Name, we pray. AMEN.

Prayer for
New Year's Day

To our Loving God, I surrender my will this year for Your Will. Your Will is so much better than mine. I have tried to live life on my own and it did not work, so God for this year, I am putting my flesh aside and I will follow Your Holy Spirit. Wherever you lead me this year, I will follow. This time of the year, the world makes resolutions and then by the time March arrives, majority of them have forgotten their resolution. Forgive me if I have done this in the past, I want a goal that I can be faithful to. So, this year- I want to follow you. I want to serve you in new ways. I want to be a faithful servant this year. Give me the courage to tell the flesh and the enemy within myself to say, no. I offer my life to you, O Lord. In Jesus Name, I pray. AMEN.

Prayer for
The Reverend Dr. Martin L. King, Jr. Day

We shall overcome today and beyond.

Precious Lord, today is a victory celebration. Dr. King, Your servant, started a revolution. He gave humankind a chance to heal the hatred against races, to open Black People's hearts to forgive whites, and for future generations to come together in unity. Through Dr. King, the world saw what a difference a young person could make. Dr. King was 26 years old when he led the Montgomery Bus Boycott. Help young people make a positive difference in their communities & churches. God, today we do not take the day off and rest, but we remember the legacy and continue to honor Dr. King's dream. God, we thank you for the presence of the 1st African-American President in the White House. But, it won't do us any good if this country is still divided - Democrats vs. Republicans. For a house divided against it self will not stand. When will politicians one day come together and serve the people of this country? We know that the different – isms in life still exists (classism, racism, sexism, and ageism). So, God help us to continue to work on these issues and not to ignore them. In Jesus Name, we pray. AMEN.

Prayer for
Married Couples on
Valentine's Day

Dear God, thank you for our relationship. Today, we are celebrating the love that we have for each other. Thank you for binding us together as one. God, you are the center of our relationship. Without you, there would be no passion between us. God, help us to continue to show our love for one another, whether it's praying for our mate, making love to our mate, or doing little things for our mate. If there is anything in our relationship, that could potentially bring us apart, please help us fix it so that we can grow closer together. Love endures all things. On this Valentine's Day, grant us more love and more desire for one another. In Jesus Name, we pray. AMEN.

Prayer for Singles on Valentine's Day

It's Valentine's Day again, already…God, how do I celebrate love today without a mate? Today, I will see couples celebrate their love for one another and I do not have anyone to call my own. The world makes people believe that if you don't have a significant other on this day, you are doomed. In a world where sex sells, sexuality is constantly being shown on the television and internet, and self-image is so important; God, help me get through this day. Help me not to feel lonely or depressed. Help me not to give into the pressure of dating. I am worth more than a desperate date. I love myself too much to date a person who only wants me for sex or cuddling. Please help me to find happiness, love and peace within myself before I look for it in others. Help me to control any sexual desires that I may have in this sex-crazed world. Valentine's Day is another day to show the love that I have for a Great God, like you. I love you, Lord today because you cared for me in a special way- way back on Calvary. You gave me a second chance. It is because of who you are, that is why I am in love with you. In Jesus Name, I pray. AMEN.

Prayer for the Divorced on Valentine's Day

Oh, Jesus…not a day for love again is it? How will I make it through this day without remembering the previous Valentine's days? I remember the good gifts that my ex-spouse gave me… now I don't have that anymore. All my married friends are going out and I am the only one staying in. Help me move past the thoughts of yesterday and help me create a better relationship in the future. In the meanwhile, help me find peace being single and divorced. Help me know that another child in your kingdom can love & respect me. I do not have to look for them, but I can wait and trust in you to find them for me. Since, I am sexually active, help me in this season to abstain from sexual activities until you provide me with a binding relationship. In Jesus Name, I pray. AMEN.

Prayers for Earth Day

To the God of all Creation, to the Sustainer Jesus Christ, thank you for providing us with a world to breathe in, to live in, and to care for. Thank you for each of the species of animals you have created. You have given us the responsibility to take care of them. Show us Your Will, show us how to take care of our environment. When we destroy this earth, we disrespect you. Forgive us for wasting your natural resources, for killing your animals, and cutting down your trees. Help us to treat the environment according to your Will and your Word. Help us to go green in our churches & communities, help us to conserve energy & oil, and help us to recycle. In Jesus Name, we pray. AMEN.

God, thank you for creating the earth and providing us with an environment that supports our daily living and gives us life every time we take a breath. Remind us that we are Your Stewards of creation and that we are responsible for taking care of the earth. Inspire us to reduce, reuse, and recycle materials where appropriate. Help us to plant gardens, trees, and to take care of the creatures of this earth. In Jesus Name, we pray. AMEN.

Prayers for Holy Week
Maundy Thursday

God, thank you for forgiving us from our sins. You used the Blood of Your dear Son Jesus Christ to make this possible. The Blood is not exclusive, but it is inclusive to all those that believe. On this Holy Thursday, we remember Jesus during the Last Supper and Jesus praying for his disciples. Thank you for the blood. Help us, to forgive those who have sinned against us. Not forgiving our enemies can cause us stress, bitterness, depression, and anger. So, continue to inspire us to forgive and not hold grudges. In JESUS Name, we pray. AMEN.

Good Friday

God, I admire Your only begotten Son, Jesus Christ today. Jesus' life exemplifies all the characteristics that I am striving for. Jesus was smart, compassionate, humble, and more. He was the sacrificial LAMB for all humankind, for that we say thank you. It was love that kept him on the cross- nothing else, but love. Thank you. Inspire us today to walk down our own Via Dolorosa's. Sometimes, we get scared of suffering, but with suffering comes a resurrection. In JESUS Name, we pray. AMEN.

Prayer for
Easter Sunday

Christ has risen indeed!!!

Through your power, God, you have given humankind new life. You have given me new life! I am free to do your will because of Christ's Resurrection. God, I want to say "yes" to your power. Resurrect the dead things that give you honor in my life. Resurrect Joy, Peace, Patience, Forgiveness, and Love… Help me know that no one can keep me down, that I will always rise again. In the Risen Savior's Name, I pray. AMEN.

Prayer for
Mother's Day

O, for a Mother's Love, is like none other...

God, thank you for all our mothers- real mothers, grandmothers, step-mothers, godmothers, and spiritual mothers; they encourage and nurture us to be the best. They taught us how to live in this difficult world. They inspired us to make a difference in our community. Some mothers have made sacrifices just to raise their children, for this we are grateful. God, comfort and strengthen our mothers. Bless them abundantly and give them peace to know that they did the best for their children. In Jesus Name, we pray. AMEN.

Prayer for
Father's Day

Mighty God, we come on Father's Day to express our thanks for the great fathers in our lives. However, some of us have had to grow up without our father and we never knew what it was like to receive love from our father. God, help us who haven't had a fatherly example in our lives. Show us tough love and be an ever-present help in our lives. God, we forgive the absent-fathers and we embrace the present fathers. Bless our fathers, grandfathers, godfathers, stepfathers, and spiritual fathers as they continue to work hard for their children and their families. In Jesus name, we pray. AMEN.

Prayer for the
Season of Pentecost

Consume us Lord, with the fire of Your Spirit. Fill our hearts and minds with the presence & power of the Holy Spirit. The Holy Spirit came to give us power to spread the gospel of Jesus Christ and to be witnesses throughout the world. Help us to continue to create opportunities to grow the Kingdom of God. The Holy Spirit not only inspires us to dance and shout, but it inspires us to live right and to make a difference in the lives of others by sharing our gifts. God, make us one through your Holy Spirit. In Jesus Name, we pray. AMEN.

Prayer for the
Military on Veteran's Day

Dear God, thank you for the military men and women who have sacrificed their time, talents, and lives for the freedom of the United States. Thank you for active military, reserve military and retired veterans who have fought in wars past. Heal and restore those who have been wounded, uplift those who came back with post-traumatic stress, and help the families who are missing loved ones. On Veteran's Day, we remember those who have sacrificed their lives and shown courage to fight for freedom.
In Jesus name, we pray. AMEN.

Prayer for Thanksgiving

We gather together to ask the Lord's Blessings…

Thank you, Lord for the blessings that you constantly give to us each day. Thank you for the people in our lives, the shelter over our heads and for the air we breathe. We do not take you for granted and we want to show appreciation for the people in our lives as we celebrate Thanksgiving. Help us to always give thanks and to give to those who are less fortunate than ourselves. In Jesus name, we pray. AMEN.

Prayers for a Wedding
For the Bride & Groom

Bind us together as one, Lord. On this day, we commemorate the love that we share for one another with the exchanging of our vows. God, help us not to take this moment for granted as we will forever look to our wedding as the symbol for our love. However, the wedding does not make the marriage. We can have the greatest wedding, but if the marriage doesn't last, it won't mean anything. Bless us as we become one, for You are the center of our lives. In Jesus Name, we pray. AMEN.

For the Parents of the Bride & Groom

Dear God, this day is bittersweet for us. We rejoice that our sons and daughters have found the one that loves them inside and out, but we also do not want to let them go. Help us to give them space and not to interfere in their new lives together. Bless their marriage and fill the void that may come when they are not around. In Jesus Name, we pray. AMEN.

Prayer for a Funeral

Dear Comforting God, be with us as we experience this difficult day. Death is not the ending, but rather a pause. It represents a new beginning to the other side. Comfort us when we miss our loved one. Help us not to hold in our emotions during the funeral, but rather we should let go of any sadness so that we can begin to move forward. Funerals are not sad occasions, but they are celebrations of life. Help us this day.

In Jesus Name, we pray. AMEN.

Chapter Three

Prayers for the Seasons in Life: Feelings

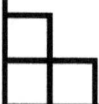

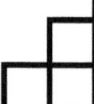

Prayer for the
Season of Rejection

God, I just feel like I am not wanted. I want to end this pain
of rejection. People have rejected me. I have been rejected in
relationships, employment, school, and church. Sometimes, my
family may reject me. Sometimes I don't go after things because I
am afraid of rejection. So, in order to not get rejected, I don't
even do things anymore. Sometimes, I get depressed and I have
thoughts about suicide. God, I need your help. God, I need your
love. Wipe the feelings of rejection away and replace them with
feelings of acceptance. God, you love me. Even though, Christ
was rejected by the world, Christ was accepted by you. Likewise,
since I am a child of God, the world may reject me, but God,
you accept me. That's all that matters! I am accepted by the
Blood of the Lamb! No matter what circumstances I've been
through; I will always know that I will be apart of your kingdom.
For this, I am grateful. In Jesus name, I pray. AMEN.

Prayer for a Fresh Start
after the
Season of Rejection

God, help me reshape my life, so that it's not built on rejection, but based on accepting. I realize that I may have rejected people and they have rejected me. So, God, forgive me each day of any hurt that I have caused in the past with rejection and I forgive those who have rejected me in the past who have caused me pain. Give me opportunities to say, **YES**, to your will. Use me each and every day to make a difference in someone else's life, in Jesus Name, I pray. AMEN.

Prayer for the
Season of Guilt & Shame

Precious Savior, I do not deserve anymore chances. I have committed so much sin, I have hurt so many people. Most importantly, I have hurt you. I feel so guilty and so much shame. How do I ever come back to you and live a righteous life? Please, Jesus, forgive me from my sins. Protect me from the evil one, so that I won't give in to temptation. You died on the cross, so that I may be redeemed and reconciled back into a great relationship with God. There is no sin that your grace and mercy will not cover, so I forgive myself today. I won't feel guilty and shameful because I am covered by the blood of Jesus. In JESUS Name, I pray. AMEN.

Prayer for the
Season of Loneliness

Dear Compassionate God, right now I am feeling lonely. I don't have many friends that I can call or hang out with. I spend time on social media networking sites looking for companionship, looking to share my life with someone. There is no one there. God, I want you in my life. Help me take away this feeling of loneliness. There is no day that goes by where I am alone. Your word reminds me that Jesus is with me at all times even to the end of the world. God, provide me with friends that I can talk to and confide in. If they are not available when I need them, cover me with your love, so that I may feel your presence. I am never alone. There is not a friend like the lowly Jesus. In Jesus Name, I pray. AMEN.

Prayer for the
Season of Depression

To the Uplifting Savior, the Rock in a Weary Land, depression is invading my life right now. The storms in my life have risen quickly, the devil has been telling me lies in my ears and it appears that there is no light at the end of the tunnel. I am so depressed. God, can you do something please? Come into my life and turn my depression into joy. Turn every lie that the enemy has told me into the truth that you have promised me in Your Word. Brighten the light at the end of the tunnel, because trouble doesn't last always. I don't have to be depressed because of the storms in my life, I can rejoice in knowing that you are able to bring me through the storms. So, it is with this faith, I will trust you. In Jesus Name, I pray. AMEN.

Prayer for the
Season of Selfishness

Dear Awesome and Giving God, thank you for giving me grace and mercy everyday. Recently, I have been putting self first, you second, and people last. I have been giving into my flesh instead of letting your spirit rise within me. Forgive me, Lord, for allowing my flesh to get the best of me. I am selfish with my time, talents, and treasure. Teach me how to be a cheerful giver, putting you first in my life. Help me to wipe away my selfishness and help me to focus on Matthew 6:33- Striving first for the Kingdom of God and for righteousness. Help me to give to others when they are in need. I desire a giving spirit, like you. In the Name of Jesus, I pray. AMEN.

Prayer for the
Season of Arrogance

To the Humble God, thank you for listening to me today.
God, I have been arrogant. I have thought too highly of myself.
At times, I thought that I didn't need to study your Word everyday. God, I need your forgiveness. Your Word says that you hate
pride. The Word also says that pride comes before a great fall. I
do not want to fall. I want to be a humble servant in your Kingdom. I realize that in comparison to you, I am nothing and you
are everything. Without you, I would be nothing. Where would I
be without your salvation, grace, mercy, and power? I cannot
even fathom. So, God help me as I become the humble servant
you want me to be. Help me not to think highly of myself. You
shall exalt the lowly. In the name of Your Humble Son Jesus, I
pray. AMEN.

Prayer for the
Seasons of Grief & Sorrow

Dear Heavenly God, my heart is filled with sorrow. Life has pushed me to the realm of sadness. I don't think I can go on like this. Wipe my tears away and ease the heaviness on my heart and spirit. I know the Word says, weeping may endure for a night, but joy will come in the morning. Right now, I'm not feeling the joy, but I know in the end the joy will come. So, God I rest in your comforting power, knowing that this sorrow will not last. It is only for a season. Help me to endure this night season so that I may give you the glory and honor when the morning comes. In Jesus name, I pray. AMEN.

Prayer for the
Season of Anger

Oh God, I thank you for being with me right now. Without you, I would probably do something that I would regret. I am reminded that I can be angry, as long as I don't sin in my anger. Help me not to sin while I am angry. I need your help to manage my anger so that it doesn't cause any harm to any individual whether physical or emotional pain. I do not need to devise a plan of retaliation for the person that hurt me; instead I need to trust you. You have my back in all situations. I desire your peace and I ask that you would quiet my frustrations. Don't let me sleep on my anger. Turn my anger into positive energy that may change the situation for the better and make a positive difference in someone else's life. I forgive the person who made me upset. In the Savior's name, I pray. AMEN.

Prayer for the
Season of Jealousy

To the Trustworthy & Almighty God, I want to thank you for providing me with the basic needs in life--- air, shelter, clothing, water, and food. I want to thank you for blessing me each and every day. Lately, I must confess that I have fallen into the sin of jealousy. I have desired something or someone that is not mine, but belongs to another. I am sorry for being jealous. I wanted it so bad. I'm sorry if I have made evil schemes to acquire another person's gifts or talents, their relationships, their money or their possessions. Forgive me, God. Create a new spirit within me that will recognize all the blessings that you give to me each day. I do not need to be jealous because you are the source of my supply. I do not need to lust over a man's wife or a woman's husband. You supply all of my needs and you bless me with most of my desires - except for the fleshly desires. You are Jehovah Jireh, My Provider. I trust you for everything. In Jesus name, I pray. AMEN.

Prayer for the
Seasons of Anxiety, Nervousness, and Worry

To the Calming Presence in the Midst of a Chaotic Storm, my life is in your hands. I am worried about how this storm will end. I don't know if I will find a job in time, or pay the bill in time. I don't know if I will survive this storm. The enemy keeps me up at night, telling me that it is over. The devil is a liar! God, I know this can't be the end. You have more planned for my life. God, thank you because I don't need to throw a pity party, but I can throw a praise party in advance. No matter what may come my way, God you are there to get me through this storm. Storms don't last always. I don't need to worry or fret because your powerful peaceful presence fills my heart, my spirit, and invades my situation. I can make it, with you I can stand in any storm. With this, I give you praise! In Jesus Name, I pray. AMEN.

Chapter Four

Prayers for the Seasons of Life:
The Human Body

Part One:
Restoration from an Illness

Prayer for the
Restoration from Diabetes

To the God of Regulation, type 2 diabetes is a problem for many people. Every day, people have to check their blood sugar, maintain a healthy diet, and do daily exercise. God, help those who suffer daily with diabetes to eat a healthy diet and help them to conquer the daily struggles of this disease. Give their body restoration power and full strength. In Jesus name, we pray. AMEN.

Prayer for the Restoration from
High Blood Pressure & High Cholesterol

Dear Jesus, the Son of God that calms our anxieties and removes stress, we call on you today to ease our blood pressure and to remind us each day to take care of our arteries, veins, and capillaries. Help us to maintain a healthy diet, avoiding overeating on fried foods, salty foods, and high sugary foods. High blood pressure can be a result of our diet, our family makeup, or our stress and anxiety levels. Jesus, help us each day as we strive to lower our blood pressure. In the same light, help us every day to take care of our heart. Without a heart, we won't be able to live and give you praise. Lower our blood pressure and lower our cholesterol, in Jesus name, we pray. AMEN.

Prayer for the Restoration from
A Heart Attack, Stroke, or Bypass Surgery

To the God who has the power to restore the heart, begin the restoration process of those who have suffered a heart attack, stroke, or have had bypass surgery. These are life threatening and life changing impurities in the body. Give them hope, courage, and inspiration to comeback from these dangerous illnesses. Show them what they need to do to prevent them from having another heart attack, stroke, or bypass surgery. God, help the people around them to invest in their new lifestyle and not cause them to slide back into the same habits that contributed to the heart attack or stroke. God, we know that you will restore them back to full health. In Jesus Name, we pray. AMEN.

Prayer for the
Restoration from Cancer

Dear God, thank you for the cancer survivors. Cancer Survivors serve as witnesses to your restoration power. When the doctor gave them the diagnosis, some might have believed it was over for them, but because of Your Grace and Mercy and healing power they are a living testimony. So, it is in this Spirit that we pray to you on behalf of the brothers and sisters who have cancer. Give them courage and motivation to defeat this disease. Remind them of your awesome strength and power. In moments of severe pain, give them a calming and soothing thought. In moments of depression, uplift their spirits. Surround them with a positive attitude and positive people. Protect them from the evil one. Cancer is not a death sentence, but it is an opportunity for you, God, to gain the glory in bringing them back to full health. In Jesus Name, we pray. AMEN.

Prayer for the
Restoration from the
Flu, Cold, and Pneumonia

To the Lord Savior Jesus Christ, we thank you for the weather that we experience everyday. Sometimes the weather overwhelms our physical bodies and we can get sick. We can get the flu, cold, or walking pneumonia. These illnesses can be minor or they could be fatal except for the cold. God, when we go through these seasons in life, take care of us. Give us all the vitamins, minerals, nutrients, and rest that we need to fight off these sicknesses. Help us to wash our hands and cover our mouths so that we won't spread our illness to our neighbors. Restore us back to full health and strength. In Jesus Name, we pray. AMEN.

Prayer for the
Restoration from Migraines & Headaches

To our Peaceful God, in stressful times our anxiety can go straight to our head and our mind. Stress can cause migraines and headaches. God, you are the God of Peace & Comfort. In times, when our body reacts to the trials and tribulations of life, grant us peace and serenity. Help us to relieve the stress and don't let it go to our head. Restore our brain when it get's overwhelmed and it acts out by causing migraines and headaches. In Jesus name, we pray. AMEN.

Prayer for the
Restoration from Sinuses & Allergies

Dear God, we appreciate the spring and summer seasons. However, with these seasons come problems with sinuses and allergies. Restore our bodies from any dust, pollen, or mold that may cross into our nostrils and cause us pain. Restore our bodies from anything we are allergic to, for example, wheat, seafood, peanuts, or dairy. God, help us to avoid substances in the earth that may creep into our bodies and give us aches and pain. Restore us to full strength and teach us how to alleviate problems from our sinuses and allergies. In Jesus name, we pray. AMEN.

Prayer for the
Restoration from Dental Work

To the Awesome God, thank you for blessing me with teeth, gums, and a tongue. The mouth is a critical part of the body. If something in the mouth hurts, it affects the rest of the body. God, ease the pain in my mouth, whether it's caused by a toothache, cold sore, cavity, gum disease, wisdom tooth, or an abscessed tooth. Provide me with the resources to restore my mouth to full health. Dental work is not cheap, so God bless me with the finances to do so. Give me the courage to endure any dental surgery, with you I can make it through. Take away the fear and give me bravery. It is in your Son Jesus' name that I trust and pray to. AMEN.

Prayer for the
Restoration from Surgery

To the God who can fix what is broken, we come to you facing a life-changing procedure. God, I know that You will be there the whole time. God, be the head surgeon during the surgery. Help the doctors & nurses stay focused, comfort me during this entire procedure. Surgery is a way in which you can restore my body. Help me to take my time to recover from this surgery. After this surgery, I will be a better me, so that I can continue to bless the Lord. In Jesus name, I pray. AMEN.

Chapter Four

Prayers for the Seasons of Life:
The Human Body

Part Two:
Struggling with Body Image

Prayers for the
Season of Obesity & Feeling Overweight

To my personal Savior Jesus Christ, today I lift up a problem that I have been struggling with- that is my weight. Sometimes I get depressed about the way I look; sometimes I eat less, and exercise more all in an effort to take the emotional pain of obesity away. To the outside world, I may not be obese, but to me I am. I need your help to take this depression and low self-esteem away. Jesus, I know that you love me just the way I am. Help me to be happy and healthy. Help me not to worry about the calories, and help me focus on loving myself. In Jesus Name, I pray. AMEN.

To the Living Savior Jesus Christ, thank you for your power in my life. Today, I am casting a care on your shoulders. I have been carrying this burden for a long time. Everyone tells me that I am overweight, and it really gets me down. People look at me and whisper mean things. Their actions have hurt my feelings. Sometimes, I get depressed and I eat constantly to get over the pain.

Jesus, I need your power to overcome my enemies. Help me to get through the depression and the hurt. Heal and restore my spirit so that I may continue to love myself. If I determine that I need to lose weight and get healthier, I will. Jesus, lift my self confidence and transform my life so that people will see that I am more than my weight, I am a Child of the Almighty God. In Jesus name, I pray. AMEN.

Prayer for the Season of Being Anemic

Dear God, I praise your name today and I give you all the glory in my life. God, I am struggling with my weight. I throw up my food in secret and I force myself to eat only a little bit each day. I try to look thin and to maintain a certain body image for the whole world. God, I come to you today because I am tired of making myself sick. I'm tired of starving myself just to stay a certain weight. God, help me to overcome this illness. God, strengthen my self –esteem so that I will eat regularly and not make myself vomit. God, help me to love myself and not to worry about what anyone else thinks of me. All that matters is that you love me and you created me in Your Image. You believe in me and that's all that matters. Help me overcome this anemia. In Jesus Name, I pray. AMEN.

Prayer for
Struggling with Skin Color

To the God who understands me and supplies my every need, I need your help. God, sometimes, I don't like my skin color because I get mistreated because of it. Or, I may not like my skin color because it prevents me from achieving some goals that I desire. God, I know that you created me for a special purpose. I need you to encourage and strengthen me. Help me to love myself; help me to love your creation. In Jesus Name, I pray. AMEN.

Prayer for
Struggling with Hairstyle

Dear Jesus, hair is so important to women. This world has stereotyped so many hair styles & colors. If a female is blonde, the world calls them "hot, sexy, and dumb." If a black man has dreads, the world may label him as thuggish and a criminal. If a black woman's hair is not done, she is not attractive. There are many more stereotypes than this, but God you understand. God, help those who struggle constantly with how their hair looks. Help them to care for their hair, but not to stress about it. Help us to do the best we can to maintain healthy hair, but God help us not to spend too much time doing our hair that we miss valuable time to serve you and to achieve your will. In Jesus name, I pray. AMEN.

Prayer for the Body Image of Under & Overdeveloped Females

Dear God, thank you for creating beautiful women. Thank you for the various curves of women and their appearance. Although, some females feel that they are underdeveloped and some feel that they are overdeveloped. The world is a cruel place. The world puts pressure on females to have large chests and if they don't they look "boyish." Most males believe a woman is attractive based on their chest size and butt size. Many women struggle with this in life. Some underdeveloped women will go to great heights to look like how men and society want them to look. God, they need to know that they are beautiful no matter what shape or size they are. God, help the females who are struggling with the lack of curves or too many curves, to know that you love them for just the way they are. Give them more self-esteem and help them not to fall into the enemy's lie, that they are not good enough or all their body was created for was sex. Females are worth more than that and they are not sexual objects. God, help them to love themselves as they are and to treat themselves with respect. In Jesus Name, we pray. AMEN.

Prayer for the Body Image of Males who Lack Muscles

Dear God, we have so many stereotypes that hurt our self-esteem and therefore cause us to struggle with our body image. For some males, we were not blessed with six-pack abs, big muscular biceps, and muscular shoulders. Some men don't want to go to the gym and bench press 500 pounds. So, God, please encourage those men who lack muscles and who look ordinary. Help them to know that you created them to do great things. Even though women are attracted to a muscular man, a man without a smart mind & spirit but who has muscles is nothing. A man who has a sound mind with a loving spirit, but lacks muscles is everything. Remind these males, that you made them. In Jesus Name, we pray. AMEN.

Prayer for the Overall Personal Look

To the Creator of humankind, thank you for taking the time to create each and every person in the universe. Thank you, for taking the time to create me. God, sometimes I struggle with my overall personal look. Some days, I don't feel beautiful or handsome. Some days, I feel like I'm ugly. God, you made me. You created me in your image. It is a challenge to live each day and feel attractive. God, help me to understand and believe that everyday that I wake up, I am attractive in your eyesight. You love the way I look and if there is something I can improve, you will let me know. I love you, Lord! Increase my self-esteem and my self-worth. In Jesus Name, I pray. AMEN.

Chapter Five

Prayers for the Seasons of Life:
The Humankind

Prayer for the Black Male

To our Powerful God, thank you for black men all across the world. Black men deal with tough issues every single day. We deal with racism and inequality everyday. Black men have to work harder and smarter than the average male in this culture. So many of our black men are incarcerated, spun out on drugs, leaders of the local gang, and are pimps of our black women. There are few black men that are positive role models for little black boys, for this reason, our black boys are on a destructive path. God, black men are MORE than pimps, womanizers, gang members, drug dealers, and criminals. God, you created black men to be Positive leaders in the community, to be faithful and pure businessmen, and to be educated and highly intelligent. God, we were chosen to lead our families and not to escape our responsibilities. God, help our black men realize and live up to their full potential. God, help us to speak encouraging words and bring life to every black male we see. God, do a mighty work in black men all across this world. In JESUS name, we pray. AMEN.

Prayer for the Black Women

To the Creative Sculptor of Black Women, we give expressions of praise and thanksgiving to you for our beautiful black women. Black Women are diverse in their skin colors- some are light, some are brown-skin, and some are dark chocolate; they are diverse in shape- some are thin, some are curvy, and some are in between. God, you created the black woman to be strong, a pillar in their families, and a sensual-smart and sexy human being. However, this world portrays our black women as lazy, music video vixens, sexual objects, and less attractive than other races. Despite beautiful black models in the mainstream media (Tyra Banks, Halle Berry, and Michelle Obama), the world still sees black women as objects and not as true beautiful spirits that you have created. God, encourage our black women when they are overlooked, when they feel down on their appearance; for they are MORE than what this world portrays them to be. God, you sculpted them to be supporters, nurturers, providers, symbols of strength and beacons of beauty. You created them to be inspirational spirits, trees to lean on, and positive & powerful sexual beings inside a marital relationship. We pray that Black Women everywhere would live up to their full potential. Continue to shine favor and peace in the lives of our black women. In JESUS Name, we pray. AMEN.

Prayer for African–Americans

Dear God, thank you for the history of the African-American race. African-Americans have been through the perils of slavery, racial inequality, and the civil rights movement… We have been blessed to see an African-American elected as a United States President; you have provided us with countless inventors, historians, social abolitionists, artists, scientists, lawyers, doctors, preachers, and counselors who have made a major contribution to the African-American community both past and present. God, continue to bless the African- American culture and race. Give us the power to continue to walk in our full potential as leaders in this world and in our community. In Jesus Name, I pray. Amen.

Prayer for Young Boys

To our Savior Jesus Christ, the One who loves all the little children, including our young boys, we offer this prayer to you. Jesus, we give our boys to you, so that you can use them to make a positive impact in this world. Take our boys away from the hands of the enemy, whether it is from negative influences, drugs, gangs, and low self esteem. Jesus, you envisioned our boys to have a positive future; a future that is filled with hope to have a great career, a wonderful family, and to be a ray of sunshine in their communities. Jesus, Your Father, our God, created boys to become inspirational men to lead future generations to come. Jesus, inspire our young boys to reach within themselves and find the great wealth that you have placed inside of them. In Your Name, we pray. AMEN.

Prayer for Young Girls

Dear Jesus, the One who was born of the Virgin Mary, we offer thanksgiving to you for our young girls. Each young girl is a representation of God's beauty and wisdom in the making. However, in the world today, girls are being mistreated and abused in many different ways. Some girls have their bodies violated and others have their self-esteem deflated because of their outward appearance. Girls are precious creatures, they should be treated with the utmost respect. Girls should not be forced to have premarital sex, to dress provocatively, nor should they be forced to go on unhealthy diets. Our God created girls to become super women who positively impact their communities. Jesus, you intended our girls to have a bright future, becoming successful mothers, having great careers, and nurturing future generations to come. Jesus, help our girls to realize they are more than their private parts, they are not objects, but creations. Inspire our young girls to reach within their spirit to find the wealth that you have placed inside them. In Your Name, we pray. AMEN.

Prayer for Young Adults

Dear Jesus, the Great Commissioner of Faith, young adult's thank you for calling us to assist you in building the Reigndom of God. We are eager to do God's Will and to be shining lights in the darkness. Jesus, there are some dark places in our lives that are blocking our light. Our dark places may include: finances, relationships, career choice, sexuality, addictions, decision-making, physical appearance, and baby mama-papa drama. Sometimes, we are so focused on finding our purpose in life, till we have missed your voice in our lives. At other times, we become so busy in life, till we leave you out of our daily agendas and routines. Forgive us, Lord. Life becomes so hectic with social media websites to entertain us each day. Lord, we want to be shining lights. Shine Your Light on our dark places; help us to maximize our potential. We are at a peak age to make a positive difference in this world, use us everyday to do Your Will. We want to be who you have called us to be. We say "YES," without any resistance. In Your Name, we pray. AMEN.

Prayer for the Adults

To the Supreme and Almighty God, we come on one accord to worship your holy and majestic name. We surrender to your power, your wisdom, and Your Will. God, at this point in life, adults have graduated from childhood and from young adulthood. Some are now carrying the baggage and the weight of the past. Some have made mistakes or experienced traumatic situations that drastically altered their lives. God, their past can not dictate the rest of their life. Free them from their past and propel them to their calling. Encourage our adults, God. Some adults are sacrificing their integrity to put food on the table and to provide for their families. God, you are Jehovah Jireh, our Provider. In Jesus Name, we pray. AMEN.

Prayer for the Senior Citizens

To the All Wise God, we offer praise and gratitude to you for the senior citizens in this world. We thank you for the life that they have lived, thank you for the dreams that they have pursued, and thank you for the many lives they have impacted. Seniors have put in the hard work to get this far and for that alone we are grateful. However, their journey is not over. In this world, senior citizens are having a tough time surviving. The world around them has changed so much; gas prices have increased, medical bills have skyrocketed, and their income is evaporating by the day. Some senior citizens are suffering from health issues, some have to go back to work because their retirement wasn't good enough, and some seniors are taken advantage of by criminals and by their own relatives. God, the senior citizens need you more now than ever before. Help them get through the stresses in life without giving up. Help them to remember that you are the same God that blessed them when they were younger and that you will STILL provide for them no matter what the age. Encourage the seniors, when they get lonely, be a friend. Spark their drive so that they will continue to mentor our young people and volunteer for charitable organizations. Help them to enjoy the rest of this journey. In Jesus Name, we pray. AMEN.

Prayer for Married Couples

To the Faithful God, the One who is first in our lives, thank you for binding us together. It was love that brought us together. God, we have been through some ups and some downs. At times, quietly, we wanted to give up on this thing, but God you kept us. When we didn't trust each other, you showed us how to trust again. When we were broke, you provided for us. When we wanted to have sex with someone else, you reminded us of our commitment. God, there are some things that we go through as a marital couple that we can't even talk about it openly. Heal & Restore those areas in our life. Help us to love each other better, not abusing each other. Help us to communicate more frequently. Help us to spend time with each other. We want to be a team working in your Reigndom. Continue to shine favor and mercy in our marital relationship. In Your Son's Name, we pray. AMEN.

Prayer for Singles

To our Best Friend Jesus, thank you for this time in my life. Sometimes, I struggle with being single, but other times I look at it as a benefit. Thank you for allowing me to explore my mind, spirit, and soul before I share it with another person. Forgive me, if I have had sex outside of marriage. Sex outside of marriage has consequences. It may result in a child, a STD, or an unwanted soul tie. Being single gets hard, sometimes I have to encourage myself. I have to pat my own self on the back. I tell myself that you have made me an attractive and awesome creature. God, I give you my singleness. Use this season of my life for your glory, in Jesus Name, I Pray. AMEN.

Prayer for the World

Dear Almighty God, we rejoice in you for creating this world. However, this world is going through turmoil right now. People all over this world are struggling in some area of their lives. Some people resort to sin to quench the needs of their spirit. That's not the answer. God, you are the source of our supply. We only need to trust you. We don't need to rob people, steal identities, hack into people's bank accounts, join gangs, or steal hair weaves from the hair store. All we have to do is fulfill our calling and you will take care of the rest. God, some of us have way too much pride and we want to provide for our families ourselves, instead of looking for outside help when we need it. Faith is there for the taking; instead we are walking by sight. God, help this world to become a better place to live in. Each day on the news, we hear of murders, suicides, and rapes. We've heard so much until our senses have become numbed to the pain and we have lost hope that things will improve. We have gotten lazy in improving our communities. Forgive us, Lord. Everyday, people hurt each other. Where is the love for our neighbor? We plot to tear down one another because we are jealous of one another.

Where is the love? Everyday, this world seems like its getting worse…we rejoice for celebrities, reality TV shows, but we don't take time to give back to those who need it until a tragedy occurs. Where is the love? God, help us to make this world a better place. It doesn't take much to improve where we live. This is our WORLD. Help us to love one another. In JESUS Name, we pray. AMEN.

Chapter Six

Prayers for the Seasons in Life:
The Unexpected Seasons

Prayer for the
Season of Job Loss & Unemployment

To the God who supplies all of my needs, I approach you this time in a difficult situation. First, I want to say thank you for my previous job and the experience that I gained from it. Thank you for my co-workers and my supervisor. God, help me not to hold any bitterness over losing this job. I realize that you are Jehovah Jireh, my Provider, and the source of my supply. The job was only the supply, not the source. God, I trust you to meet my financial needs until you lead me and direct me to my next job. Help me to manage and budget my resources correctly. Don't allow me to stop looking and applying for work. Keep my confidence level high. Giving up is not an option. If I have to reinvent myself, please order my steps and give me a vision and a plan. Above all, I will trust you; you're the SOURCE of my SUPPLY. I give my job loss to you. Hear my cry, in Jesus Name, I pray. AMEN.

Prayer for the
Season of Homelessness

To the One who gives us shelter during the storm; thank you for being by my side every waking moment. For some reason, I no longer have a home to live in. God, this is not what I expected. There has got to be more to life than this. God, please make a way out of no way and provide a permanent place to stay in. Whatever resources, I may need open the doors, so that I may be able to walk through them. God, help me in the meantime to remain patient and persistent. I trust you, that you will supply my every need. In Jesus name, I pray. AMEN.

Prayer for the
Season of Accidents

To the God I adore, thank you for sparing my life after what just happened. God, I couldn't have made it without you. Help me in the times when I flashback to this accident. Let Your comforting and consoling Spirit, be with those who were effected by this accident. God, you haven't brought me this far to leave me here. I'm still here, still standing in the midst of it all... Help me to recover from this accident and protect me as I recover from this. In Jesus name, I pray. AMEN.

Prayer for the
Season of Weather Damage

Dear God, the Shelter in the time of the storm, you promised that you would be with me in the storm and in the rain…so God, I know you are here. Just a few moments ago, everything was fine and now the storm has damaged my property- whether it is a building or a car. Lord, help me get through this difficult time. Replace everything that was lost and help me not to panic. As long as I am still alive, we can replace the material things. Thank you, for letting me survive the storm. In Jesus name, I pray. AMEN.

Prayer for the
Season of Crime

To our Protector and Comforter, theft, rape, assault, and everything in between are crimes in this world. Gangs are formed to threaten our communities and destroy our livelihoods…Sometimes, "lone wolfs" commit crimes out of hatred, negativity, and jealousy. Sometimes, everyday people commit robberies because they have an inward desire to provide for themselves, but God this is not the answer. We know robbery is not the answer because God, you are our Provider. God, for the countless people who have been victims and witnesses of crime, restore their mental and emotional beings. Experiencing crime is a traumatic event. Restore the possessions which were loss in the crime committed three-fold. Speak life into their wounded hearts and be a shield of protection for them. God, I know this world won't ever be perfect, but with you, we can strive for a world without senseless crime. God, you are able. In Jesus name, we pray. AMEN.

Prayer for the
Season of Tragedy & Death

Here in this moment, gone the next moment…

To the Comforting God, when tragedy strikes, time is still. The pain is so overwhelming, that we don't know what to do. We don't know how to handle the severe pain of sudden loss. We were expecting our loved one to live a long life and for it to end, like this, Wow! We don't understand the timing of death, why it has to come so quickly…God, help us in this hour of grief and tragedy. Allow us room to vent our emotions to you, as long as we do not sin. Mend our broken hearts and comfort us, when we mourn. Help us not to hold our sadness in, but to turn our sadness into a beacon of hope. Encourage us when we feel down. In Jesus Name, we pray. AMEN.

Chapter Seven

Prayers for the Seasons in Life:
For our Leaders

Prayer for the
President of the United States of America

To the Almighty and Powerful God, thank you for entrusting us with Presidential Leadership in the United States. We do not take the Office of President for granted. God, the Office of President is very challenging. The President has to deal with two to four political parties, left and right government media, the affairs of this Nation, and the relationships between other countries and the United States. God, bless our President, our First Lady, and their families. Encourage them everyday as they encounter stress-filled situations. Inspire the President's Cabinet and Staff, including the Vice-President and the Secretary of State, to assist the President, to do the best they can each and every day. Keep our President safe from all hurt, harm, and danger. Fill his mind with positive voices and not the negative critics. Give the President innovative ways to revitalize this country and economy. God bless the President of the United States of America. In the name of Jesus, we pray. AMEN.

Prayer for the Government Officials

To the God who specializes in unity, bind our government officials closer together. As a country, we won't be able to achieve excellence in the economy with divided government officials. The United States have three or four parties trying to have power in the government. They are the: Democrats, Republicans, Independents', and the Tea Party. Help our government leaders serve the people in their constituency with no hidden agendas. Help our leaders to remember in their political decisions the working poor, the working middle class, and future generations who fight each day to survive in an ever-increasing, price-consuming world. God, it is written in Your Word, that a house divided against it self cannot stand. So, God if the United States wants to stand in the economy, education, energy sectors, and as a Nation as a whole, our government officials need to put aside their differences and act on one accord. Only, then will we be able to stand together as a nation. In Jesus Name, I pray. AMEN.

Prayer for
Clergy & Ministerial Leaders

To our Living and Powerful God, thank you for calling men and women all over the world to preach the Gospel of Jesus Christ to others. In this day in age, some clergy and ministerial leaders have become distracted. Some are more focused on the problems that they face, instead of focusing on the faith that they possess. People look up to preachers for guidance and direction. They look for them to provide stability in their lives. God, this is a dangerous situation. God, only you can provide stability and guidance within our lives. God, help our preachers and pastors to maintain their integrity in a world that seems to lose integrity every day. Show them new ways to do ministry. In Jesus Name, I pray. AMEN.

Prayer for
Church Leaders

To the Awesome God, who leads us and guides us every day, thank you for placing leaders within your churches. Church Leaders, such as- Stewards, Trustees, Deacons, Presidents, Lay Workers, and Youth Leaders are very important to the function of the ministry and the building of your Kingdom. Without effective leadership, a church can rapidly fall into confusion and chaos. God, entrust the people who hold leadership positions with active minds, compassionate hearts, and with ears that listen to everyone. Keep them from becoming prideful and arrogant because they have an authoritative position. Help them to delegate responsibilities and help them to remember that the follower is just as important as the leader. Give our leaders new dreams that support the purpose of the church. Give them the plan that will help them make those dreams into realities. God, people are hurting and we need humble leadership to help restore the people who are hurting. In Jesus Name, we pray. AMEN.

Prayer for
College Deans, Principals, & Teachers

Thank you, God for all of the teachers, principals, and college deans within education systems all across the world. These leaders within our community provide valuable lessons to our children and young adults. Teachers motivate our children to find their passion in life and they lead them into that direction. Principals govern our teachers and our students, so that should negativity come into the atmosphere, they can pour positive power within their lives. College Deans constantly make a difference in the lives of their faculty, staff, and students. God, encourage our teachers, principals, and college deans to continue to teach positive lessons to the students they teach. When they grow weary of the daily routine, give them motivation to complete their tasks on a daily basis. In Jesus Name, we pray. AMEN.

Prayer for
Police Officers & Firefighters

To the Chief Protector, thank you God for keeping us safe in the midst of crime and fires. We want to pause and say thank you for blessing this world with brave police officers and courageous firefighters. Police officers, risk their lives every day to keep communities safe from hurt, harm, and danger. Thank you, God for their strong ability to capture people who have hurt others by their actions. God, be by their side every day, bless them with discernment and give them courage when they are scared to death. Thank you, for firefighters who battle fires every day, keeping communities safe from the flames. God, help them to be unified when they fight fires and save lives. Bless their families, as they struggle daily with the concern that they may never see their loved one again. We love you, God. Keep our police officers and firefighters safe from all hurt, harm, and danger. In Jesus Name, we pray. AMEN.

Chapter Eight

Prayers for the Seasons in Life:
Starting a New Life

Prayer for
High School Graduates

Dear Jesus, thank you for bringing me through the challenges and trials of high school. It wasn't easy; I thank you for listening to every prayer I prayed and for good teachers along the way. Now, I'm leaving the familiar for the unknown. Bless my classmates as they go on their separate ways. Help me, as I meet new challenges and discover the new "me" inside of me. Provide me with the resources that I need to make it through higher education and plant within my heart the pathway to the life that you want me to live. In Your Name, I pray. AMEN.

Prayer for
College Graduates

Hallelujah! I Made It! I survived!

Thank you, God for my new degree. God, you have heard my cry over the last few years and thanks to your ability, we made it! Now, God over the years I have become familiar with the routine of college. Adjust my mind to the real life. Help me to use the education that I received to make a difference in someone else's life. Graduation is not the end; it is just the beginning of living in the real world. God, you have blessed me with knowledge; bless me with the ability to act off of that knowledge, but by your spirit alone. Encourage my friends as they depart for their own journeys. Walk with them as they embark on their new lives after college. In Jesus name, I pray. AMEN.

Prayer for
Breaking Drug Addiction

Dear God, I have the desire to stop using drugs. However, my attempts have failed. Now, I am seeking Your power to help me break this drug addiction. At first, I thought I wasn't addicted, but now I realize I am. Drugs have ruined my relationships with my family, my friends, and they have wreaked havoc on my finances. I need your Power & Grace! Help me, now God. Come into my life and reshape my mind and spirit. God, I want to stop using drugs. Help me to breakaway from the enablers to my addiction. Give me a support and accountability network to check on me everyday until I finish recovering from this addiction. Help me to live a healthy lifestyle in the meantime. This won't be easy, the devil will tempt my mind and body, but God keep me away from the evil one. Protect my rehab and recovery period. I believe that with you, God, I will be able to overcome and break my drug addiction. I surrender to your Power! In Jesus name, I pray. AMEN.

Prayer for
Breaking Sexual Addiction

Dear God, the Creator of Sexuality & the Inner Spirit, I come to you to admit a difficult addiction that I have. I love sex. It feels so good. I can't stop myself from having it, or watching it. I recognize that I spend too much time with my sexual nature and the sexual nature of others. Just praying this prayer, is very hard. You know, watching television is hard. There are so many sexual innuendos in every program. God, I just want to break my addiction to sex today! I know it won't be easy in this sex-crazed culture, but I know with you all things are possible. Instead of looking for a sexual partner all of the time, I want to experience a relationship that has more features...a relationship that stimulates the mind, spirit, and soul. Sex only lasts for a moment, but has lifetime consequences. I am thirsty for something everlasting. So, God help me break my addiction to sex, which includes pornography and hooking up! God, build a support group of people around me that will hold me accountable on this daily journey. Eliminate the temptations, and protect me from the enemy. In Jesus name, I pray. AMEN.

Prayer for
Breaking Internet Addiction

To the All-Knowing God, thank you for invention of computers and the internet. Lately, God, I have spent way too much time on the internet. God, help me to cut down on the time that I spend on the internet. I think it prevents me from serving you effectively. Also, I admit that I have disconnected myself from real people and I have connected myself with social profiles and fake avatars. I fill my time playing online games for hours and hours, instead of studying Your Word and improving my relationship with you. Lord, help me to break my addiction to the Internet. There is more in the world that you want me to see and discover. So, God enlarge my territory and provide a positive support group around me to help me break this. I Love you, Lord more than anything and I will do anything to serve you. In Jesus name, I pray. AMEN.

Prayer for a New Career

Dear God, thank you for where you have brought me in my life so far. Now, God as I get ready to embark on this new journey, be with me every step of the way. My desire is that this new career will bring you glory and that I will be able to make a positive impact in the lives of other people. Help me to earn enough money in this career to pay off all of the debt I have incurred over the years in preparation, to pay off all credit card debt if I have any, to take care of the necessities in my life, and to give to others. I will remember to keep you first by tithing ten percent to my local ministry. Without you, blessing me with this new career, I wouldn't be in this awesome position. I love you, God and you come first. In Jesus name, I pray. AMEN.

Prayer for a
New Baby in the Family

To Jesus, the one who loves little children, we are expecting a new human being into our family. Thank you for blessing us with a new bundle of joy. With this joy, comes a new responsibility. We have to teach the baby right from wrong and to encourage them to find their place in this world. Jesus, bless the baby to have a successful childhood. Lead the parents to nurture the child and to take care of them properly. Give the baby and their parents all the things they need. Surround the baby with a whole lot of love from family, friends, and neighbors. Jesus, give this baby favor to do your Will and not our will. In Your Name, we pray. AMEN.

Prayer for
Forgiveness after Sin

To the God of another Chance, I come to you requesting forgiveness for the sins I have committed by thought, word, and deed. I acknowledge that I have made a huge mistake and I need your forgiveness. Wipe the slate clean and help me get off to a fresh start. Your forgiveness allows me to forgive others when they hurt me, reject me, or ignore me. When someone persecutes me, I should not hold a grudge against them. Rather, I should forgive them just like you forgive me. God, you forgave me and gave me another chance to do Your Will. Thank you, God for this New Chance. In Jesus name, I pray. AMEN.

Prayer for Salvation

Dear Jesus, you caught my heart, my mind, and my soul. Jesus, I did not believe in you, but something happened. Someone took the time to show me the Christ in them. After that moment, I wanted you in my life. Jesus, I don't want to live another moment without your salvation and your steering hand in my life. To Jesus and to God, I believe that Jesus was crucified on the cross, died, was buried, and that Jesus rose on the third day. I believe that Jesus is coming back again. The blood that Jesus shed on the cross was enough to save a wretch like me. I love you, Jesus. I want you to be the Savior in my life. In Your Name, I pray. AMEN.

Prayer for
Recommitting my Life to Christ

I strayed away from you, Lord. I struggled to pray to you, Jesus. I wanted control of my life. Now, I realize that living my life away from you wasn't the greatest decision. Now, I want to reignite my relationship with you, Jesus. Without you, I am nothing. I am recommitting my life to you. Reveal to me the plans and the visions you have for me. Bring me back to you and closer to you, in Jesus name. I pray. AMEN.

"After We Pray"

The Conclusion of the
Book of Prayers for the Seasons of Life

I hope you enjoyed the prayers throughout this book, whether it was a biblical prayer or an inspirational prayer; but the work is not done. There is work to do after we pray. It is not enough to just pray. We have to get up off our knees and put some action behind our words. The bible says, Faith without works is dead! So, a prayer without actions behind it is dead. We may believe in the prayer we prayed, the song we sung, but if we don't do anything to get our desired prayer request, our prayer request will become delayed until we do something. For example, if we ask God for a quality job that can provide benefits and a healthy wage in a great location, but don't seek out opportunities and apply for them...we will continue to wait for the request to be answered. Most of the times, God is waiting for us to answer our prayer.

Now, sometimes God will say NO to our prayers for any reason. God is God and God has the power to direct and guide our life and has the right to say no to our prayer request. When God does say no, it is either not the time for the prayer request to become reality or the request is not in God's plan for your life. God still loves us, even when God says no to us.

It is our job to trust God enough after we pray, that God will move on our behalf and do more than what we asked or imagined God would do.

After we pray, let's get up off our prayer request and move into an action position. Let's listen for God's voice and be ready to move when God speaks. Prayer changes things.

***

My Personal Prayer to God

_____

_____

_____

_____

_____

_____

_____

_____

_____

_____

_____

"If my people, who are called by my name, humble themselves, pray, seek my face, and turn from their wicked ways, then will I hear from heaven, and will forgive their sin and heal their land."
2 Chronicles 7:14 (NRSV)

www.ingramcontent.com/pod-product-compliance
Lightning Source LLC
Chambersburg PA
CBHW071137090426
42736CB00012B/2147